ANIMAL SPIRIT GUIDE

POWERFUL GUIDED MEDITATION TO FIND AND CONNECT WITH YOUR ANIMAL SPIRIT

ADESH SILVA

CONTENTS

Introduction   5

1. The History of Animal Spirit Guides   9
2. What is An Animal Spirit Guide   26
3. Why Am I Searching For A Spirit Guide?   31
4. How to Find Your Spirit Guide   36
5. Guided Meditations   54
6. Honoring Your Spirit Animal   70

Conclusion   79
References   81

© **Copyright 2020 - All rights reserved.**

The content contained within this book may not be reproduced, duplicated or transmitted without direct written permission from the author or the publisher.

Under no circumstances will any blame or legal responsibility be held against the publisher, or author, for any damages, reparation, or monetary loss due to the information contained within this book, either directly or indirectly.

Legal Notice:

This book is copyright protected. It is only for personal use. You cannot amend, distribute, sell, use, quote or paraphrase any part, or the content within this book, without the consent of the author or publisher.

Disclaimer Notice:

Please note the information contained within this document is for educational and entertainment purposes only. All effort has been executed to present accurate, up to date, reliable, complete information. No warranties of any kind are declared or implied. Readers acknowledge that the author is not engaged in the rendering of legal, financial, medical or professional advice. The content within this book has been derived from various sources. Please consult a licensed professional before attempting any techniques outlined in this book.

By reading this document, the reader agrees that under no circumstances is the author responsible for any losses, direct or indirect, that are incurred as a result of the use of the information contained within this document, including, but not limited to, errors, omissions, or inaccuracies.

INTRODUCTION

In nearly every major culture throughout history there has been a common belief that we travel through life with the assistance of a group of spirits helping guide us. Arguably the most prolific of these beliefs is the animal spirit guide. An animal spirit guide is a wealth of wisdom and knowledge that any person is capable of tapping into but very few actually take the steps towards doing so. In this book I hope to teach the wonderful benefits of having an animal spirit guide and the great improvements it can bring to both your life and your all around health and wellbeing.

Throughout the chapters of this book you will learn about the old practitioners of spiritualism, where around the world these practices were performed throughout history, and the impact that the belief in animal spirits may have had on modern day culture. We will explore what an animal spirit guide is, the various types of guides we may run into, and the meanings of each type of animal spirit. We will journey into all the techniques we can use to find our guides and what your discoveries may personally mean for you. Lastly, we will go into detail on guided meditations which will allow us to communicate with our guide, and we will learn how to honor the bond we have with our spirit guide. The relationships we have with our guides are integral parts of our lives and should be treated with the right amount of respect and love.

Keep in mind much of this book is what you make it to be. It is up to you, the reader, to put the effort and energy in to make something of all this information. It may seem like a daunting task, and it certainly will not be a short process. However, if you are looking to grow as a person, there is no better place to start than with a journey to find your animal spirit guide. These tentative first steps into spirit animals, totems, and your bond with the natural world may seem scary at first, since they involve exploring parts of your spirituality that you did not know existed before, but they will enlighten you more than you could ever imagine and will allow your spirit to soar.

1

THE HISTORY OF ANIMAL SPIRIT GUIDES

As with many great spiritual concepts, the animal spirit guide has its roots in ancient man. We are not talking about some 2000's social media trend; this is an ancient, tried, and tested belief which has withstood the test of time and has graced many of mankind's greatest cultures. As well as influencing ancient man, the concept of animal spirit guides has had an influence on the modern day. Our ancestors' belief in the importance of the animals in the world around them means the world we live in today is completely different to the world they left behind.

A HISTORY OF ANIMAL SPIRIT GUIDES

Throughout human history there have always been beliefs that not only do we have a soul, but that everything in the living world around us has a soul as well. Regardless of whether you look to the beliefs of Native Americans, Sub-Saharan tribes, or Shinto practitioners in Japan, that is a common theme that all of them share. Through ancient text and art we have a portal to the past that allows us to see and understand so much about our ancestor's beliefs. Unfortunately most of our history on this earth has been lost to us, but we can piece together some details through these relics. A very well documented belief among our ancestors was that of a living animal guide or an animal spirit guide. These concepts have differences that will be examined later, but their shared purpose was to provide guidance and wisdom to ancient people.

The reverence that ancient man had for the animals around them can be seen in places like Lascaux, a network of caves in southwestern France, where some of the most comprehensive and well preserved examples of ancient artwork ever discovered can be found. In these caves there are countless depictions of aurochs, buffalo, lions, deer, and horses, all painted carefully onto the walls by Paleolithic man. This respect for the creatures around them was born from the reliance ancient man had on them and the understanding we shared with them. Humans were not always the top of the food chain; we shared fears and struggles with many of the creatures around us, which led to bonds between people and the animals that they lived and survived with.

You may ask "How does this tie in with spirit guides?" and perhaps it does not. I just find the relationship we had with the natural world to be fascinating. I think it is possible that the reason our ancestors revered these animals so much is not simply from an appreciation for food. There was almost certainly a great spiritual significance to the cave paintings of ancient man. Many believe that our ancestors did not necessarily worship the animals around them, but rather felt at one with them. They may have seen humans and animals as equal parts of a greater whole. This spiritual connection is what the basis of our beliefs comes from. We still share this bond with the world around us. When something dies, that bond is not broken but rather grows stronger.

ANIMAL SPIRIT TRADITIONS AROUND THE WORLD

For millennia, and in every corner of the globe, humans have in some way revered animal spirits. This reverence took place among the San people of Southern Africa, the Australian Aboriginals, and Incan shamans in Peru. Regardless of where you are, chances are your ancestors, or at least the native people of that land, had spiritual guides in the form of animal spirits that were significant to their culture.

Africa

In nearly all African cultures we will find revered animals, or totems, that are culturally significant to each and every tribal group. These totems are important animal spirits that offer protection and guidance to the tribes, and in return the spirits and living animals receive protection and offerings. Some tribes could have more than 100 different totem animals which they would live in harmony with, if one of these animals was to be found dead, the tribe would hold a funeral ceremony and help its spirit join its kin.

The San people of South Africa, Botswana, Namibia,

and Angola make up the first nations of Southern Africa. They are the original, ancient inhabitants of the region, and many of them still practice forms of spirit animal meditation and trance rituals. In San religion, for a shaman to enter the spirit world he must hunt a totem animal, typically the eland, and free its spirit from its body. Once the hunt has been completed, the shaman will then use the fat of the Eland in a ceremony which will grant them access to the spirit world.

The Zulu people of South Africa revere cattle greatly in their traditional culture. In Zulu tradition if a white calf is born to a commoner, it should be immediately gifted to the king. White in Zulu culture symbolizes purity, harmony, and a closeness to the divine, so cattle of that color have massive ritual significance to the Sangomas (diviners) and Inyangas (healers) of the Zulu people. The Sangomas may choose to perform a ritual sacrifice of the cattle to free its spirit and, in turn, gain its wisdom and help.

The Hausa people of West Africa are primarily Islamic in their current beliefs, but still have syncretic elements of their pre-Islamic animist culture. In pre-Islamic Hausa culture, priestesses would perform rituals in which they allowed spirits, be they human or animal, to possess them and speak through them. Whether these were acted out vision quests or actual possessions we may never know, but the importance of animal spirit guidance is plain to see. Only a handful of traditional shamans still practice these rituals.

The Serer people of Senegal believe in an ever present class of spirit called the Pangool. These spirits can be anything or anyone, but their primary role in Serer religion is as a guardian and messenger of the divine being. Although the Pangool are often seen as ancestor spirits, animal spirits are just as common and act as guides sent by the Gods. The Serer view these animal spirits as extended relatives of human beings, and believe that all souls came from the same holy womb.

The traditional religion of the Kikuyu people of Kenya suggests that every living creature has a vital force given to it by the supreme creator. The vital force of every creature has a particular strength, so a man may have a stronger force than a bird, but a weaker force than an elephant. One can increase their vital force by using something of smaller vital force as an intermediary. This does not necessarily mean through consumption or sacrifice; simply taking something of lower force into your protection is enough to increase your spiritual standing.

Probably the most famous African religious culture of all is the Egyptians. Egyptian religion is a very long and complicated rollercoaster ride, so it is not a surprise that somewhere along the lines they discovered animal spirits. When asked to picture Egyptian Gods many people immediately think of Thoth, Anubis, or Ra with their animal heads, which is not a coincidence. These gods were thought to act through their animals, so these animals and their spirits were thought of as divine. If you were to care for a divine animal you would gain the favor of the spirits and in turn the favor of their God.

Asia

Asia is the world's largest continent and has a near uncountable amount of local religions and cultures. Most of these belief systems are syncretic with Hinduism, Islam, Buddhism, Taoism, and so on. However, despite their adoption by larger organized religions, the vast majority of asian belief systems share a common factor in their reverence of animal spirits and their belief in respecting nature.

The Chinese Zodiac is a wealth of knowledge for someone getting into animal spirituality and as such, it is something we will cover in detail later in the book. But the zodiac is just one important aspect of how animal spirits have influenced Chinese culture and folklore. For example, many people have seen a Lion or Dragon dance on television or the internet. This popular form of Chinese parade dance consists of multiple dancers donning the same large Lion or Dragon costume and performing as one flowing, living being. Many people do not realize that traditionally when the dancers start the dance they are not viewed as only performers. They welcome the spirits of the dragon and lion into them, and allow these spirits to act through them. This performance exists to bring luck and good fortune by honoring the spirits of these great Zodiac spirits.

The Dravidian tribes of Southern India's traditional religion revolves around Animism, which is the belief that all creatures around them have a soul. It is common in Dravidian folklore to attribute certain qualities to the souls of these living things, such as strength in the ox or nimbleness in the stag. Rituals are performed in which someone can eat the flesh of these creatures to take on their attributes and hope to improve themselves.

In the Shinto religion, which is practiced by up to 80% of the Japanese population, the Kami are a group of spirits which represent elements of the landscape and nature. The Kami are not separate from nature in Shinto folklore, but rather of nature, meaning that they inhabit the bodies of fauna and the matter of flora. Every Shinto follower strives to be in harmony with nature so as to be in harmony with the Kami.

Europe

When many people think of religion in Europe, they think of organized Abrahamic religion, mainly Protestantism and Catholicism. But Pre-Christian Europe was truly a melting pot of dozens of unique Polytheistic religions, many of which were based around nature spirits and a respect for the natural world.

The ancient Celts were at one point the most widespread and populous group in Europe, their people's reach spanning from the Black Sea to Portugal, from the north tip of Scotland down to the Mediterranean. Much of Modern Druidism and Paganism is heavily based around the beliefs of the ancient Celts. These beliefs revolved around the sanctity of nature and its spirits. For many Celtic sects, various animals were believed to possess spirits with certain qualities. The snake was seen as a symbol of enduring life and renewal. The badger was a symbol of bravery and unyielding courage in the face of danger. The stag was seen as a guide from the spirit world that could lead you into contact with a higher being. Each one of these animals had a spirit which the Celts believed would bless them with the qualities of the animal, if they appealed to its spirit.

In Finnish mythology, every species had an "Emuu", a spirit which inhabited every animal of a species. Before a hunt, hunters would pray to the Emuu of the animal they wished to hunt as a form of respect to the spirit and to ask for a favorable hunt. The bear and elk were particularly important animal spirits to the Finns. They were often portrayed as equals to man in their standings in nature. The Finns also revered the spirits of water birds, and the swan in particular. It was believed that because of the swan's long neck, it could see into the spirit world and communicate between our world and theirs. Finnish shamans would therefore often call upon the swan spirit as a messenger to the other side.

The Norse religion is a particularly well known example of Pre-Christian European religion. Like all other great ancient belief systems, the Norse had a plethora of animal spirits that were integral to their mythology and folklore. These spirits were called Fylgjur and inhabited the bodies of companion creatures. A Fylgja is tied to the spirit of its owner; if the owner dies so does the Fylgja. The Fylgja that an individual may have is based on their character. A strong person of noble birth may have a great bear, an intelligent and cunning person may have a raven, or a hardworking and dutiful farmer may have an aurochs.

North America

Pre-Columbian North America was inhabited by a massive number of Native American tribes spread throughout the entire length and breadth of the continent. Each tribal group had unique pantheons of Gods and spirits, many of whom had prominent roles in day-to-day life. The hunter-gatherer lifestyle of most of these tribes meant that these spirits were often observed in the form of animals and plants important to each tribe.

Animals such as the seal, polar bear, and narwhal were revered as important spirits to the people that inhabited the harsh landscape of what are now Alaska and the Canadian Northern Territories.

These animal spirits were often called upon by shamans in the hope that their tribal hunting parties would have favorable hunting and their settlements would be protected from the elements and wildlife.

In Iroquois mythology, every single animal has a unique soul but none are more sacred than albino stags, boars, and buffalos. In the modern day we know this is albinism, but for the six nations of the Iroquois a white animal meant a message from the spirit world. Any white animal was to be followed as they were believed to lead a person, or their tribe, to great things. The spirits of these creatures were treasured so highly that it was thought to bring terrible luck upon not only yourself, but the entire tribe, if you were to kill such a creature.

Further to the south lay the lands of the Apache, Navajo, and Pueblo tribes. These were hardy people who inhabited the desert and arid plains of modern day Texas, New Mexico, and Arizona. These tribes do not have many particularly recognizable animal spirits, but they do include the coyote extensively in their folklore. The coyote is viewed as a mischievous spirit who is just as likely to harm as they are to help. In many Native folk tales the coyote is a key figure, either leading the protagonist astray or helping them through devious means.

Oceania

The Australian Aboriginals are one of the oldest surviving examples we have of religious society in modern man. They are made up of hundreds of different tribal groups who for the last 50,000 years have inhabited the Australian continent and some of its smaller surrounding islands. The world in the eyes of Aboriginal Australians is one that is constantly moving; everything is alive and energized by a spirit. Humans in their religion are an equal part of nature and are morally obligated to treat animals, plants, and the landscape around them with respect. In their beliefs the spiritual world and our world are not separate, so your actions at all times may influence how the spirits around you greet your presence. Each family, clan, or tribe has a set group of totem animals and plants which they are duty bound to look after. The spirits of these fauna and flora will in turn bless their caregivers. Every person has a totem animal. When an aboriginal is born, the first encounter their mother has with an animal determines their totem. It is understood that the spirits of the nearby land, fauna, and flora gave life to you, and therefore you owe them your service in return.

The Maori reside across the Tasman Strait in New Zealand. They are a great warrior-like people whose own pantheon and mythology has been built up over thousands of years of migrations and wars. Maori mythology features the concept of *Mana*. Mana is a term used to describe great power in a person or animal. It is intrinsically linked to the strength of your spirit. A person with a lot of Mana is destined for great things. Mana is present in animal life, not just humans, and it is common for tribes or individuals to adopt guardian animals based on the perceived strength of the animal's Mana. A dog with a distinct birthmark or a shark with a particularly prominent scar could be perceived as creatures with Mana. Such creatures would deserve respect and protection, and in return their protectors will be blessed by the spirits.

South America

Every single native pre-Columbian tribe across the South American continent practiced some form of animist religion. These tribes included the Inca high in the Andes Mountains, the Mapuche in Patagonia, and the various jungle tribes strewn across the

Amazon basin. They all shared in common a great respect and love for the land around them, which carried over to the animals that they shared that land with.

The Incan Empire was the largest empire in pre-Columbian America. A great part of their strength and success as a unified people was their religious practices, which focused on harmony in the home and nature. The Incan people revered three great animal spirits as core entities in their religious beliefs.

The first of the three was the condor. The condor was viewed as the most sacred bird of the Incan people. This massive bird of prey is able to fly incredible distances, and because of this the Incas believed it to be a messenger of the heavens and a guide to the lost. Incan tales tell of armies who followed the condor through shortcuts in the mountains in order to surprise their enemies.

The second spirit animal of the Incan people was the puma. The puma was a symbol of strength and ferocity in Incan society, and was revered by all Incans. Being the greatest predator and the only true hunter of men in the region made the puma something to emulate, which led the Inca to build their cities and forts in the shape of a puma.

Their last spirit animal was the snake, which represented rebirth, renewal, and the wisdom which comes with age. Incan shamans would often keep snakes in their places of ceremony and use them to help with future prediction ceremonies.

THE IMPACT OF ANIMAL SPIRIT TRADITIONS ON MODERN CULTURE

You may wonder how beliefs in animal spirits have influenced modern culture. The thought that these ancient, even prehistoric, beliefs have a direct effect on our lives today is pretty absurd. But let me explain and soon you shall see the logic behind this idea.

What is one thing that many of us share in common with each other in our home? Some of you may have grown up with it; almost all of you will have a friend with one. Do you have no idea what I'm talking about? It's a pet!

Dogs and Cats, in particular, are the most common pets worldwide. Of course, there are many reasons for the popularity of pets over the centuries, but it is fair to suggest that originally the concept started as a form of spirit animal companion.

Wolves were some of the first animals to be domesticated. In addition to serving as a great hunting tool, they were venerated as powerful spirit animals by nearly every people that shared land with them. It makes sense that these people would give offerings to wolves as a way to appease the spirits and in turn they, over time, domesticated the wolves. Cats too were domesticated very early on and a similar logic applies. Cats have always been viewed as intelligent and cunning creatures. Many cultures believed they had ties to the spiritual world and some saw cats as protectors against malicious spirits. Again, it makes perfect sense that people would seek to keep these animal spirits close and appease them with offerings.

Aside from pets, the belief in animal spirits by many tribes led to the preservation and protection of many species of animal that otherwise may have died out due to overhunting. The bison, for example, was a powerful spirit animal to many tribes of the Great Plains region. It had a flourishing population until Christians arrived in the region and began large-scale hunting of the bison.

2

WHAT IS AN ANIMAL SPIRIT GUIDE

From a purely spiritual standpoint, an animal spirit guide is an extension of your own spirit. It is an untapped source of power and inspiration in most people, and an invaluable resource in life for those who have accessed it. This spirit, in a way, mirrors your own spirit: you share traits, characteristics, and the same goals in life.

WHAT ARE ANIMAL SPIRIT GUIDES?

An animal spirit guide is, in essence, a teacher that comes to us in the form of an animal which we have a personal connection to. An animal spirit guide can reach out to us in many ways, including through dreams or a physical encounter. Regardless of the method, they exist to share wisdom, protection, and guidance with us, and in return we cherish and protect them.

TYPES OF ANIMAL SPIRITS

There are various types of animal spirits, and a person may have multiple guides depending on their strength of spirit and level of enlightenment.

- The life animal guide is your primary spiritual guide. This guide reflects your own spiritual self and shares an unbreakable bond with you. Even those who do not believe in animal spirit guides have a life animal. By recognizing this guide we open ourselves up to the spiritual world and reveal an extension of our own soul. This guide is constantly protecting and looking out for you. Think of it as a guardian angel. It exists to share knowledge with you which can, quite literally, save your life.
- Bird guides are some of the most important guides we may hope to run into. They symbolize a transition into new stages of life, provide knowledge of things possibly above

us or out of our spiritual capabilities, and have incredible knowledge of events that may happen in our future.
- Reptile guides are crucial for those of us looking for a change in life. They represent adaptability and transformation. They are also independent and show great wisdom about all things concerning personal growth.
- Insect guides give us wisdom and patience. They are guides for those of us who seek a long term goal and are not afraid of taking our time in life. They show great tenacity and progressiveness in any object they work towards. Like an ancient river carving out a canyon, they work slowly yet consistently towards a goal.
- Mammal guides are linked to the earth. They give us a sense of grounding and humility. A mammal guide is needed for anyone searching for greater mental and physical stability. With a mammal guide comes great intuition and situational awareness as you become much more communal and aware of social situations around you.
- Water guides represent a need for independence and freedom. They embody

the free flowing nature of the world around us, and remind us that to live you must keep moving forward. Water guides are particularly adept at revealing wisdom to us through dream states and the subconscious mind when our brain is at its most free.

THE DIFFERENT GUIDES

Aside from the different origins of our guides and what they may mean, every guide shares a different purpose to us that can be totally independent of their species.

The Journey guide is an animal guide which comes to us when a life changing decision approaches us. When we need to make a big decision on our future or the direction of our life, this guide may show itself to us. This spirit will help us through the important journeys of personal growth that we undertake, and will help us make the right choices at that time for ourselves. It represents the journey of spiritual growth and the rewards which come with positive change.

The Messenger or Teacher guide is a spirit which appears to us when we are in desperate need of guidance, whether we know it or not. This is the most persistent of all our guides and will continue returning until it is understood and acknowledged. This spirit may show us moments from our past which we need to learn from in order to succeed in future tasks. This guide may also bring foreboding warnings.

The Shadow guide is arguably the most powerful guide in your life and is the greatest source of personal growth. This spirit guide will appear to you as a manifestation of your fears and anxieties. It reminds you of the parts of yourself which need to be healed and your flaws that need to be overcome. It may appear in the form of nightmares and troubling visions, but it exists to help you and fighting against it will not make it go away. This spirit is persistent and will return until it sees change. This guide will continue changing throughout your life and pushes you to constantly better yourself.

3

WHY AM I SEARCHING FOR A SPIRIT GUIDE?

Every person pursues a spirit guide for their own reasons. Many of us feel a draw towards this topic and we cannot explain it. I highly recommend that you take a bit of time to lay out some goals and hopes for yourself. Having a plan for what you hope to accomplish in life, both in the distant future and near future, and writing a list of improvements you wish to make to yourself will help focus your power toward the change you want. Remember your spirit animal is an extension of you. Your goals are their goals, and if you know what you want then they will too.

WHY DO WE BELIEVE IN ANIMAL SPIRIT GUIDES?

Personal beliefs aside, I think there are some fantastic reasons to believe in animal spirit guides even if it is just conceptually and not spiritually. Animal spirit guides can be thought of as a tool of the subconscious mind to those who are unsure of their belief in spirits. We can look to the natural world and recognize characteristics in the creatures we see that we wish to emulate in ourselves. Our mind is incredibly powerful and we barely understand a fraction of the things it is capable of. It is possible that everything we experience is just a figment of our mind. But that does not make any of the dreams we see, feelings we experience, or ideas we have any less real. Likewise, thinking about our spirit animal guides does not make them any less real.

HOW CAN MY GUIDE HELP ME?

Many people may question the need to find your animal spirit guide. I've stated some good reasons in passing so far in this book but it boils down to one simple question: Do you wish to grow as a person? For anyone seeking spiritual and emotional growth, finding your spirit guide can be a massive step towards self-improvement. A theme of many Native American tribes is bettering oneself to better the world around you. By improving yourself you can strengthen your bond to the spirits and the world around you. Your growth helps everything around you improve. Finding your guide can also be a source of inner peace. Many of us have restless souls. We constantly bounce from one thing to the next not really knowing what we hope to achieve in life. By opening yourself up to your animal spirit guide, you open yourself to the potential of finding your path in life. Your guide may lead you in the direction you've needed to travel this entire time. A spirit animal may bring clarity to your mind and help you focus your energy towards a single goal. Of course, aside from the benefits of having an animal spirit guide, the process towards discovering and communicating with your guides is therapeutic and healthy for us too. We will dive into guided meditation later in the book. It is a fantastic way we can deal with stress and unwanted emotions.

LIVING WITH MY ANIMAL SPIRIT GUIDE

Aside from the long term benefits of personal and spiritual growth, having an animal spirit guide brings its own day-to-day perks. Animal spirit guides bring a unique form of companionship. For the most part they will not be physically present, but they are always with you and that is a very warming and wholesome feeling of comfort. When you are visited by one of your guides, you can be sure that the occasion is important. During experiences like that you will feel an incredible surge of spiritual satisfaction. Your mental health can benefit massively from having a spirit guide as part of your daily routine. They exude a calming presence which can help in the work environment. The meditation techniques we will come to later are also a great outlet for releasing stress and anxiety in your everyday work. Of course, our spirit animals act as a form of inspiration for us too. We can look to our animal spirit guides during the day as a reminder of the qualities we want to emulate. If your work day has been particularly long and hard, take a minute to picture your animal spirit guide in its natural environment. Note its qualities and how it approaches life with ease. This may help inspire you to approach your aspects of life with a similar confidence.

4

HOW TO FIND YOUR SPIRIT GUIDE

We've gone over the history of animal spirit guides, including where they were believed in and where they may still be believed in. Now it's time to add your home to that list. In this chapter, you will learn how to find your spirit animal. Keep in mind that you do not pick your own spirit animal; your guide chooses you. Go into this with a clear and open mind, and be welcoming to whichever animal spirit guide chooses you.

HOW TO DISCOVER YOUR ANIMAL SPIRIT

Discovering your animal spirit is actually a rather simple process. These spirits are not exactly discreet in the hints that they give, so you probably already

ANIMAL SPIRIT GUIDE

have an idea of the spirit you may be tied to. Regardless of whether you think you know or not, you should take an initial leap toward discovering your animal spirit. That leap is rather simple: you just ask. Ask for the animal spirit to show itself at the start of each day until you feel its presence. You may leave the house to go to work someday and find a raven pecking at something on your driveway. While at work, a coworker may mention the Baltimore Ravens' latest score or draft prospects. On your commute home, someone on the car radio may mention *The Raven* by Edgar Allan Poe. When you get home, you may turn on the television and see the National Geographic channel has a documentary on ravens. I think at this point it would be pretty obvious that this particular spirit is reaching out to you.

THE VARIOUS TECHNIQUES YOU CAN USE

Aside from asking, there are some other techniques you can use if your animal spirit is being a bit too subtle with their signs. It is completely possible that your guide has attempted to get your attention in the past through events in your life, animal encounters, memorable connections, dreams and nightmares, or even the zodiac sign you were born under. All of these can factor into what your animal spirit guide may be, so some thinking back to your past may reveal many things to you.

Past Connections

Significant connections are one of the clearest and most obvious signs that your guide may give you. Did you have a favorite animal growing up as a child? Did your family have any strange pets? Maybe you've always felt drawn to a particular animal, or there is always an animal you make sure to visit at the zoo or aquarium. These connections, no matter how small they may seem, can be big hints towards what your guide is.

Encounters

Reviewing my past encounters is how I found a large clue towards what my animal spirit guide may be. I remember playing in a neighbor's yard as a child. One of us accidentally kicked our ball over to an old clothesline in a now overgrown part of the yard. I went over to fetch the ball. As I approached the clothesline, I heard a very faint ruffling sound. I looked up to see a large spotted eagle owl looking down at me with piercing orange eyes. Since that encounter, I have been called up at random at a show in a bird sanctuary to hold that same species of Owl. When I lived on a farm a whole family of them nested nearby on the property. The coincidences are uncanny considering the owl was a favorite animal of mine when I was a child.

I suggest you think back into your own past to try to figure out if you have had any encounters that stick out to you, and whether any creature has made multiple appearances in your life. An animal that you frequently see near your home or that takes particular interest in you may be a sign from your guide. It is even possible that if you were attacked or bitten by an animal in your past, that experience may have been a test put forward by your guide.

Dreams

Dreams can be a powerful form of communication between you and your guide. More often than not, you may receive hints and messages from your guide in the form of dreams containing certain animals. Asking your guide to appear to you before going to sleep at night may trigger the dreams you need to discover your animal spirit guide. Daydreaming can also reveal hints to you. You may find your mind wandering during the day and when you snap yourself out of it, the one remaining image you have could be that of an animal. If you catch yourself zoning out during the day while fixated on a picture on the wall, perhaps that picture has an animal in it that was drawing the attention of your subconscious mind.

Fears

It could be that a certain animal has always scared you. You feel anxious just thinking about this animal, but you cannot exactly figure out why. You may be fascinated by this creature but also totally repulsed by the thought of it. It is a commonly held belief by many Native American tribes that the animal which you fear most may be the creature which allows you ascension to your next step of enlightenment. Overcoming your fear and embracing this animal may allow you to grow as a person in ways you could not imagine before.

Zodiac

There are various different types of astrological zodiacs which have been used throughout history, but only a few of them specify an animal spirit link. Two zodiacs that merit a detailed examination of their animal connections are the Native American zodiac and the Chinese zodiac.

The Native American zodiac is deeply linked to the land and animals of the North American continent. If you are from North America I would highly recommend you explore this zodiac in detail. The Native American people put a lot of importance into the seasons when developing their zodiac split it into four seasonal quarters. Those four quarters are split into a further 3 pieces each. When placed together into a circle formation, the zodiac creates a medicine wheel. The circle is an important sign of unity and continuity in Native American astrology. The animals and birthday ranges of the Native American zodiac are:

- **The Goose. December 22 - January 19:** The Goose is the first animal of the Native American zodiac. This graceful creature represents action and a willingness to go to great lengths for success. The Goose is the sign of ambitious people who are never afraid to journey outside of their comfort zone in order to achieve what they want. In terms of personal life, the Goose represents loyalty and structure. Geese may put much

time into nest building and creating a perfect environment in which to flourish.
- **The Otter. January 20 - February 18:** The Otter is the second sign of the Native American zodiac. Otters are complicated and impetuous animals and these traits carry over to those born in their month. These individuals are always looking for unusual ways to solve the issues that surround them and their loved ones. Otters are incredibly communal animals that live their lives in small communities surrounded by family and friends, to whom they are fiercely loyal. Intelligent and curious creatures, Otters tend to explore the world around them and constantly learn from their surroundings.
- **The Wolf. February 19 - March 20:** The Wolf is the third sign of the Native American zodiac. Wolves cherish independence but care deeply for their pack, which can make them come across as contradicting at times. The Wolf represents strength and keen awareness of your surroundings. These individuals rely on blazing trails forward for themselves and the other members of their pack. They are never

afraid to take a leap of faith. Someone blessed by the Wolf may find themselves particularly attuned with the world around them and can receive clear and insightful wisdom through observation.

- **The Falcon. March 21 - April 19:** The Falcon is the fourth sign of the Native American zodiac. Falcons are fast acting and confident creatures that are completely sure of their own capabilities. Falcons are typically leader types and competitive in their approach to life. In their personal life, Falcons are supportive and intense. They can be abrasive at times but that stems from their drive, and want, to see others succeed around them.
- **The Beaver. April 20 - May 20:** The Beaver is the fifth sign of the Native American zodiac. Beavers are diligent and industrious workers; their drive towards a goal is admired by all around them. Unstoppable in their work ethic, those blessed by the Beaver will constantly seek out a new challenge to test their limits. In the home, Beavers are caring and considerate. They pride themselves in safe and harmonious

relationships and are happy to help uplift those they care for.

- **The Deer. May 21 - June 20:** The Deer, also known as the Stag, is the sixth sign of the Native American zodiac. Deer are elegant and regal creatures. These social and sensitive individuals excel at social situations and naturally attract people with their magnetic personalities. Those blessed by the Deer have a natural affinity for bringing others together, and may find themselves acting as mediators during tumultuous times in their personal lives.
- **The Woodpecker. June 21 - July 21:** The Woodpecker is the seventh sign of the Native American zodiac. Those born under this sign are renowned for their heart and compassion. This sign is tightly tied to a connection to the mother earth and Woodpeckers show that mothering spirit to all those around them. Empathy, compassion, and support are words that define this sign. Those blessed with the Woodpecker spirit are natural protectors and have the protection of a powerful spirit.
- **The Salmon. July 22 - August 21:** The

Salmon is the eighth sign of the Native American zodiac. This animal spirit represents energy and enthusiasm. Those born under the Salmon have a restless drive to progress in life. Although thought of as selfish at times because of their drive towards personal goals, Salmon are uplifting to those who share their vision of life and can be a great steering force in those who they keep around them.

- **The Bear. August 22 - September 21:** The Bear is the ninth sign of the Native American zodiac. This imposing animal represents strength and a quiet, distant view of life. Bears prefer solitude and observe life from a careful distance, only moving forward once they have seen all they feel they need. In their personal life, Bears are warm and accepting, albeit introverted.
- **The Raven. September 22 - October 22:** The Raven is the 10th sign in the Native American zodiac. Those blessed by the Raven are natural diplomats, capable of being endlessly charming and impartial. These individuals relish the fast paced nature of the world and love working under

pressure. Ravens base all their decisions, whether personal or businesslike, on educated points and well-done research.

- **The Snake. October 23 - November 22:** The Snake is the 11th sign of the Native American zodiac. Those born with the Snake are adept at adaptation and are able to change their perspectives in life very easily. These individuals are very fluid and flexible emotionally. In Native American tradition the Snake is closely linked with shamans because of their ability to heal and regenerate. People blessed with the Snake may find their presence around others to be emotionally healing.

- **The Owl. November 23 - December 21:** The Owl is the 12th and final sign of the Native American zodiac. Those blessed with the spirit of the Owl are observant and seek knowledge in every aspect of life. These individuals have a zealous desire to uncover secrets and hidden wisdom which often leads them to ask the bigger questions in life. The vision and wisdom of the Owl also brings with it optimism and understanding

about how to approach situations in life, the
Owl is always prepared.

The Chinese zodiac, unlike the Native American zodiac, is based on a twelve year cycle rather than a twelve month cycle, with each year in the cycle relating to an animal sign. In the Chinese zodiac it is believed that each of these animals has a lucky meaning and can guide those born in their signs to their personal goals. Each animal has certain traits which it is believed carry over to the people who are born in the animal's year. It is often considered good luck to revere and honor your year animal in China. The animals and birth years of the Chinese zodiac are:

- **The Rat:** If you were born into one of these years you are blessed with quick wits and an ability to improvise under pressure. These individuals are resourceful and versatile, always able to make the best out of any situation. Rats are also known for their kindness and communal nature, keeping a large support structure of friends and family around them. The years of the Rat are as follows: 1936, 1948, 1960, 1972, 1984, 1996, 2008, and 2020.

- **The Ox:** The traits Oxen are famous for carry over well to those born in these years. Oxen are known to be diligent and hard working. They are never afraid to get their hands dirty to get a job done well. These individuals are resilient and dependable, and are always ready to help out those in need of a strong hand. The years of the Ox are as follows: 1937, 1949, 1961, 1973, 1985, 1997, 2009, and 2021.
- **The Tiger:** Those blessed with the traits of the Tiger are a force to be reckoned with. Ever brave in life, they are not afraid to charge headlong into any challenge. Their confidence is a dominant feature that extends beyond their appearance and into their work and art. Tigers are fiercely competitive which shows clearly in their preference to be athletes or artists. The years of the Tiger are as follows: 1938, 1950, 1962, 1974, 1986, 1998, 2010, and 2022.
- **The Rabbit:** Those born in the year of the Rabbit have a quiet and kind nature. These people tend to keep to themselves and focus

on their own goals going forward. Rabbits are also characterized by a strong sense of responsibility and duty. These individuals are not likely to take their tasks lightly and can be trusted to finish what they started. The years of the Rabbit are as follows: 1939, 1951, 1963, 1975, 1987, 1999, 2011, and 2023.

- **The Dragon:** Those blessed by this noble creature exude an almost regal confidence in the way they approach life. Dragons are characterized by their wisdom and love for challenges, therefore those of this year will often find themselves drawn to situations where a keen mind is needed. Enthusiasm is also a dominant feature of these individuals. They are always ready for the next step in their personal journey. The years of the Dragon are as follows: 1940, 1952, 1964, 1976, 1988, 2000, 2012, and 2024.
- **The Snake:** The traits of the Snake are very cerebral. These individuals are known for their enigmatic and intelligent nature. They rely on their wits and wisdom to guide themselves and others forward in life. The Snake also represents renewal. Those of this

year show an incredible ability to change aspects of their life on a whim. The years of the Snake are as follows: 1941, 1953, 1965, 1977, 1989, 2001, 2013, and 2025.

- **The Horse:** Energy and activity surround those born in this year. These individuals are in a constant state of movement from one place in life to another. Their restless and energetic spirit is infectious and those around them will take inspiration from the endless vigor of the Horse. The energy of the Horse should not be confused with recklessness though, as people of this year show a gentle and careful nature. The years of the Horse are as follows: 1942, 1954, 1966, 1978, 1990, 2002, 2014, and 2026.
- **The Goat:** Those born in the year of the Goat are known for their calm and rational minds. They are well suited to handling precarious situations with ease. Their calmness and rationality carry over to their treatment of others. Goats show incredible sympathy and give off a presence of comfort. They make excellent diplomats and mediators due to their impartiality. The

years of the Goat are as follows: 1943, 1955, 1967, 1979, 1991, 2003, 2015, and 2027.

- **The Monkey:** This playful and mischievous creature displays itself very clearly in the people born to its year. Monkeys are curious and smart. They are adept at problem solving and problem creating. Life with a Monkey nearby is never boring. Despite their mischievous nature, these individuals also show a caring and nurturing attitude to those close to them. The years of the Monkey are as follows: 1944, 1956, 1968, 1980, 1992, 2004, 2016, and 2028.
- **The Rooster:** Quite the opposite of chicken stereotypes, the Rooster is a brave and fearless creature. Roosters approach life with their heads held high. They are ever observant of the world around them and ready to react swiftly. People of this year work tirelessly to build a safe environment around them and the ones they love. Roosters pride themselves in having harmonious relationships with those around them and are quick to remove harmful energies. The years of the Rooster are as

follows: 1945, 1957, 1969, 1981, 1993, 2005, 2017, and 2029.

- **The Dog:** Those born in the year of the Dog are loving and loyal souls. Ever prudent and forward thinking, they are exceptionally adept at leading households or communities. You should not take their kindness for naivety: Dogs are very intuitive and insightful. The years of the Dog are as follows: 1946, 1958, 1970, 1982, 1994, 2006, 2018, and 2030.
- **The Pig:** In Chinese folklore the Pig does not possess the negative image it has in western cultures. In China the Pig is a symbol of compassion and generosity. Those born to the year of the Pig have a tender and liberal nature. They are always willing to explore new things in life. Pigs are often the first to break new ground and pave the way for others to follow. The years of the Pig are as follows: 1947, 1959, 1971, 1983, 1995, 2007, 2019, and 2031.

WHAT YOUR GUIDE MEANS FOR YOU

Regardless of what zodiacs, articles, or blogs may say about your animal spirit guides' meaning, it is up to you to decide what your guide truly means for you. It is fully up to your own interpretation. I recommend taking some time for introspection after discovering your spirit guide. Try to figure what you want this guide to empower in you. With a clear idea of what you hope to achieve and work towards, you can fully utilize the tools that your spirit guide will give to you.

Do not fret if your animal spirit guide is not what you were hoping for. Many people want something powerful like a bear or noble like an eagle, but every animal spirit guide has its own unique positive traits. It is imperative that you keep an accepting viewpoint and stay patient. Learn everything you can about your spirit guide and you will discover a deeper meaning that satisfies you.

5

GUIDED MEDITATIONS

In this chapter we will explore meditation, an ancient technique used to unlock the hidden power of our mind. Through meditation you will be able to open your mind, communicate with your spirit guide, and access your subconscious mind.

The oldest documented use of meditation is among the ancient people of the Indian subcontinent from approximately 5000 to 3500 BC. The first written evidence of meditation was in the Vedas, a collection of Indian holy texts, around 1500 BC. Of course, meditation has probably been around as a concept as long as man has acknowledged the heavens and the spirits. Meditation has been used by nearly every culture and religion in some way. Celtic druids would chant prayers around great bonfires, Native

American shamans would bang drums in hypnotic rhythms while singing to the spirits, and even Christian monks would spend hours on end in quiet, repetitive prayer, in the hopes of receiving some divine inspiration.

WHAT IS A GUIDED MEDITATION?

A guided meditation is a step-by-step process of connecting with the spiritual aspect of the world around you. These forms of meditation have been used for millennia as quick rituals that one can perform at any time of day and in any environment. The point of guided meditation is to give the mind a single task to focus on. Your brain tends to wander, which can make it troublesome for you to find the focus you need in order to communicate with the spirit world. By having a path laid out for you to travel, you can remove the need for your mind to wander. You will find plenty of examples of spiritual guided meditation online and I highly recommend you try them all out. I will include some fantastic guided meditations in this chapter to give you an idea of the magic of these forms of meditation.

Before We Start

Before we get into any meditations, I feel I should state that you may not immediately feel the effects of meditation. This is common for many people starting out and should not discourage you. You will feel the benefits over time with more practice.

To experience the connection with your spirit animal and the benefits which come from it, you will need to stay conscious and awake. Try to choose a position that is comfortable, but not so much comfortable that you feel yourself dozing off. Sitting upright in a chair, kneeling on a pillow, or sitting cross-legged are favorites for many people. These positions will allow your body to relax yet stay awake.

An important thing to remember when preparing to meditate is keeping an open, passive mind. Allow your mind to relax instead of forcing it. Experience the feeling without trying to control it. Let things take their course naturally. It is perfectly normal to have stray thoughts pop into your head while you are trying to meditate, but don't let them agitate you. Acknowledge them and send them on their way by focusing on the topic of your meditation.

An important initial step when preparing to meditate is finding the right place. It is possible you will not always be in the same place every time you want to meditate, so make a list of requirements that you can apply to multiple places. Comfort and peace are very important to a successful meditation, so try to find a place that is quiet and out of the way. Everything else is up to your preferences. An example list of requirements for a place of meditation may include:

- Outside or with a view of the outside.
- Good lighting, preferably sunlight.
- Clean and uncluttered.
- Comfortable seating.

Once you have an idea of your ideal meditation environment, you can decide on a place to do your first guided meditation. Fulfill the requirements on your list and make sure you feel cozy. There is no dress code for meditation so any clothing will be fine; just make sure you feel comfortable. Loosen any scarves or ties and kick off any heels or tight shoes.

Before any meditation, it is wise to switch off all technology around you. Your phone, in particular, is a massive distraction and should be removed from your meditation environment.

A GUIDED MEDITATION TO FIND YOUR SPIRIT ANIMAL

Before we begin, seat yourself comfortably in your chosen meditation position. Take a moment to think of a short phrase that you will use to call upon your spirit animal. This phrase can be anything you feel will work. For example, you might use "Come forth my guide" or "Reveal yourself to me." By now you should be comfortable. You can make small adjustments while you meditate but try not to move too much.

Let us begin.

Close your eyes. Start relaxing your muscles. Clear your mind. If any thoughts come forward, think "clear" or "blank" and turn your attention back to relaxing your body.

Your muscles will slowly become loose and relaxed. Start with your toes, your feet, and your ankles. Flex them and relax.

Focus on your calves, your thighs, and your pelvis. Feel the muscles in your legs loosen.

Move your focus to your stomach, chest, arms, and back. Feel your abs relax, your chest slowly rise and fall with each breath, and your arms go limp in relaxation.

Think about your shoulders, neck, and face. Feel your shoulders drop, your neck release all of your built up tension, and your facial muscles let go of all emotion. Your body is at peace.

Focus now on your breathing. Notice each breath without changing your breathing. As thoughts come, just disregard them and focus back on your breathing.

Breathe naturally and deeply. Inhale for three long seconds, exhale for three long seconds.

Again, disregard any thoughts, clear your mind, and focus on your breathing.

With a clear mind, think of your special phrase. Every time you exhale, I want you to repeat that phrase in your mind.

If your mind wanders at any point in this session, just repeat your phrase.

Passively, you will feel yourself drifting. With every breath you feel yourself float further into relaxation.

Now we will count down from five to zero. When

we reach zero, you will be in the deepest state of relaxation you have ever felt.

Five. You take a deep breath in, holding it for a second, and repeating your special phrase you exhale.

Four. Your mind is clear and welcoming. You feel yourself drifting further into relaxation. Breathe in, hold it, and release.

Three. You breathe in, hold, repeat your phrase, and release. You can see your phrase drift out into the void. As if it is a message in a bottle, moving into an endless sea.

Two. You are at peace. The only thing in your mind is your phrase. Breathe in, hold, release.

One. Breathe in, hold, repeat your special words, and release. You hear your phrase faintly echo back to you. As if you are being called to as well.

Zero. Stay here in peace for a while. Breathe and repeat your call. If your spirit animal wishes to appear, they shall do so soon.

Slowly you begin to become aware of your body again. Your shoulders slowly rise, your fingers

ANIMAL SPIRIT GUIDE

stretch, your back tightens, and your leg muscles become alive again.

Notice your breathing, still calm and slow. You are becoming more aware of your environment.

Slowly you open your eyes, letting them adjust to the light. Sit quietly for a moment, enjoying the feeling of peace as your body slowly awakens.

Think about your experience and take in everything you felt.

If you saw an animal, it may very well be your spirit animal. If you did not, that is fine too. For the best results and clearest answers, you must always meditate on a subject multiple times. Return to this meditation again and you may find different results.

COMMUNE WITH YOUR ANIMAL SPIRIT IN MEDITATION

Before we begin, seat yourself in your chosen meditation position. Take a bit of time to picture your animal spirit guide. Imagine them in their natural environment. For example, if your spirit animal is a bear then imagine them in a great, green forest. Take your time and settle yourself until you feel ready to meditate.

Let us begin.

Take a deep breath. Close your eyes and exhale.

Breathe in through your nose and out through your mouth slowly and deeply.

Let your chest rise and fall. Feel the cool, fresh air flow into your lungs. Every breath makes you feel more relaxed.

You feel a wave of relaxation flow through your body, starting at your fingers and toes.

It flows back and forth, each time flowing further, reaching through your legs and arms now.

Still breathing deeply, you feel the waves of relaxation reach your shoulders and chest.

With every wave you feel your body release its stress.

The waves reach your neck and head now. Your eyebrows relax and your neck releases tension. You are totally relaxed.

Now take another long, deep breath. Inhale through your nose and exhale through your mouth.

Picture yourself in your animal spirit's natural environment. You can feel the sun on your head and shoulders as a slight, warm breeze blows past you.

You can smell the environment around you. Take a deep breath in through your nose. The air is fresh and clean. Exhale through your mouth.

Imagine a pathway ahead of you lightly lit up by the sun. It glows warmly as it weaves its path forward.

You travel down this path slowly, taking a deep breath with every step. As you travel, you observe the beautiful environment around you.

You come towards the end of the path, where you find a large, comfortable pillow basking in warm sunlight. You take a seat on this pillow and feel yourself sinking into it.

As you sit there, warm and comfortable, you feel a presence.

Call to your spirit animal now. Picture them in your mind.

Welcome them forward. They may approach slowly or appear right beside you.

Continue your deep, slow breathing. Spend a moment in silence with your spirit animal.

Breathe in and out. Now ask your spirit guide to speak with you.

Let them share any wisdom they wish to. Pay close attention to their movements, the way the environment around them moves and changes.

You can see the words your guide speaks written out in your mind. Take note of them.

Now you feel light, almost as if you are being pulled up by the warm breeze.

You stand and your guide leads you to the edge of the large circle of sunlight you have been sitting in.

Your guide crosses out of the light and slowly disappears. You feel a sense of happiness.

Slowly, you start acknowledging your physical body again. Starting with your toes and fingers, you feel them twitch.

Moving up through your arms and legs, you feel the muscles flex gently.

Your eyes slowly open and take in the room around you. You breathe again, deeply.

Think about your experience. Write down everything you saw and felt. For the best results and clearest answers you must meditate on a subject multiple times. Return to this meditation again in the future and you may receive even more wisdom.

TAKING A JOURNEY WITH YOUR ANIMAL SPIRIT GUIDE

Before we start, seat yourself in your chosen meditation position. I want you to form a mental image or picture that represents something you need guidance for. It can be anything. For example, maybe you need advice on an important choice in your career, or you need help with a personal relationship. A career choice could be represented by picturing your workplace, while a personal relationship can be represented by picturing that person or something that reminds you of them.

Let us begin.

With your picture in mind, allow yourself to relax. Take a deep breath in, hold it for two seconds, and exhale.

Let all your tension melt away, as you fall further and further into relaxation with each breath.

Take another deep breath in, hold it for two seconds, and exhale. Empty your lungs completely.

As you continue to breathe like this, you are already beginning to drift into a state of deeper relaxation.

Bring your attention to the top of your head. Feel the relaxation flowing down from the top of your scalp.

Let your eyebrows and ears relax. Breathe in and out.

Let your mouth and jaw release their tension.

This flow of relaxation spreads further down into your neck and shoulders. You feel the stress leave these muscles.

Breathe in and out.

Let this feeling of total relaxation spread through your chest and arms, all the way to your fingertips.

While your body relaxes, so does your mind. Your thoughts float away and your mind becomes totally blank except for your picture.

The feeling of relaxation now flows through your stomach and spine. You feel the muscles in your back relax as you inhale and exhale.

This warm feeling of calm continues to flow down through your pelvis and thighs. You feel the muscles of your legs release their tension with every breath.

Calm flows through your knees, calves, and into your feet.

Your entire body and mind is in a state of total relaxation. You feel calm and at peace.

Imagine that you are seated on the most comfortable pillow you could ever dream of. This pillow is soft and warm. It wraps itself around you, and you feel completely at peace.

You look up around you to see that you are seated on a cloud. The sky above you is painted in beautiful shades of purple, blue, and red.

As you gaze around, you see that you are surrounded by an endless sea of light, fluffy clouds.

You feel at peace here. A warm and light breeze blows past you.

As you enjoy the warmth of the wind, you notice that a light mist slowly surrounds you.

With every breath you take you feel more relaxed. The mist quietly rolls in.

Recall your picture now. Imagine holding it in your hands as a photograph.

Ask for your guide to join you. Welcome them out of the mist, and into the clear air in front of you.

Notice that the mist in front of you parts as your guide passes through.

You are now together, at peace, in this beautiful place.

Show your picture to your guide. Tell them what you wish to have their wisdom for.

Watch carefully as your guide shares their knowledge with you. Listen and observe.

Spend some time with your animal spirit guide. Be in their presence, in complete harmony.

The mist slowly creeps in again, and your guide passes back through into the fog.

The sky above you starts to change shades slowly,

becoming more orange and yellow, eventually fading to a light blue.

The mist starts to fade away. The sun shines on you, warming your limbs.

In time you will feel yourself awakening again to another wave of relaxation.

The wave creeps its way back up through your feet, calves, and thighs, warming and waking you as it travels.

You feel the flow of relaxation reach your stomach and back. You notice your breathing again.

The wave reaches your chest and arms. You become aware of your fingers again, and they twitch slightly.

The wave flows through your shoulders and neck to the top of your head.

Your eyes carefully open, and you become aware of the room that you are in.

You feel a deep sense of satisfaction with your experience.

Take a few minutes to readjust before you get up again.

6

HONORING YOUR SPIRIT ANIMAL

Now that you have met your animal spirit guide, you can start growing your relationship with them. A strong relationship is important. As your bond with your guide strengthens, you can expect your communication to improve with them. You may see your guide visit more often and take a greater role in your life if you allow them to. A stronger bond with your guide also means a stronger bond with the mother earth and nature, and only good can come from that.

HOW TO HONOR YOUR SPIRIT ANIMAL

Honoring your spirit animal is a great first step towards building your relationship. This can be done in many ways, so feel free to try them all and decide what works best for you and your guide.

- Make a small shrine for your guide. Cover it with photos, statues and other tokens of your spirit animal.
- Wear clothing or jewelry depicting your guide. A bear paw necklace, eagle feather earrings, or even just a shirt with a wolf on it can bring you closer to your guide.
- If possible, visit a place where animals of your guide's species live. Watch them in their natural habitat, and spend quiet time around them. Visit a zoo and see if you can have a hand in feeding the animal. If your spirit animal is not native to where you are, get a hold of a DVD or some videos online and be with your guide in that way.
- If your guide's species is endangered or protected, consider donating to charities to help protect those animals. You could also sponsor the animal at a nearby zoo or conservation area.
- Read books about your spirit animal. Research them and learn their habits, characteristics, and native habitat.

- Write an essay, poem, or story about your spirit animal. Putting work into something which honors them is always appreciated and is a sincere form of thanks.
- Take part in actions which honor the spirit of your guide. For example, if your guide is a dolphin, learning to surf may bring you closer to them. If your guide is a bison, ox, or bull, weightlifting and increasing your raw power may be appreciated.
- Do something to conserve your animal's native habitat. This can be something as simple as cleaning up litter on the beach or at the park, or something more advanced like donating to anti-deforestation charities. A whale person may donate to ocean cleanup organizations. A tiger person may pay for a tree to be planted in a forest.

GROWING THE BOND BETWEEN YOU AND YOUR GUIDE

All of the things listed above will help grow your bond with your spirit guide, but the most important thing that you can do is talk to them. Communicate with them daily if possible. Only communicating with them when you need something is not a very healthy way to treat the relationship, so daily meditation sessions and prayers will go a long way towards strengthening the connection between you and your guide. Keep in mind that these meditation sessions do not need to be conversational. Of course, you can feel free to share anything with your guide, but it is perfectly fine to just sit in silence with them.

UNDERSTANDING YOUR RELATIONSHIP WITH YOUR SPIRIT GUIDE

Your relationship with your guide is a precious one that only you will ever really understand. It is important to remember that this relationship is symbiotic. You are both equal parts who equally benefit. Do not fall into the trap of worshiping your guide. They are not deities. Recognize them as humble spirits who are here to help you and work with you. Respect, honesty, stability, mindfulness, and diligence are the words you should look to when thinking about this relationship you have and what it stands for.

Treat your guide as an old friend. Be kind to them, help them, and offer them warm greetings every time you meet. They will grow to become an incredibly positive influence in your life if you sow the seeds well. You can take the things you have learned from this relationship and transfer them into the outside world too. Apply these values to your other relationships and watch as the world around you flourishes.

AN HONORING GUIDED MEDITATION

Communicating with your guide is an important part of your relationship with them. In this guided meditation I will give you a short example of what kind of meditation you can do during your day to spend a spare five to 10 minutes with your animal spirit guide.

Seat yourself in your preferred meditation position and place your hands on your stomach.

Let us begin.

Start by taking a few deep, calming breaths. In through the nose, hold for three seconds, and exhale through the mouth.

Continue breathing deep. In through the nose, hold for three seconds and exhale out through the mouth.

Continue this rhythm of breathing. Feel your

stomach rise with each breath. Feel the cool air fill your lungs and circulate throughout your body.

Imagine the air rushing into your lungs with each breath. Every time you inhale, you feel lighter and calmer than before.

Breathe in, hold for three seconds, breathe out.

Imagine yourself sitting in a beautiful and green clearing in the woods. Tall pine trees tower over you, giving you shade. A warm, fresh breeze blows by your shoulder.

In the middle of this clearing is a large pillow. You walk over to this pillow and take a seat. It is warm and impossibly comfortable. You feel yourself sinking into it, totally at peace.

Breathe in, hold for three seconds, breathe out.

You notice now, for the first time, a hedgerow in front of you.

You feel a familiar presence beyond the hedge. It is your spirit animal guide. Call them forward.

You see the hedge slowly part as your guide travels through it into the clearing before you.

Take your time to appreciate the beauty of the creature before you.

Now ask your guide if there is anything you can do for them. Ask if there is any way they may appreciate being honored.

Listen carefully and observe their actions. If your guide has anything to say, they will share it now.

Spend time with your guide, here in this clearing surrounded by nature. Enjoy their presence.

Let the feeling of gratitude and love that you have for them radiate from you.

With every breath you take, you spread that feeling of love to your animal spirit, and further grow the bond between you.

When you are ready to say farewell to your guide, smile and thank them for coming.

You see the hedge behind them open once more and your guide passes through.

Gently you stand from your pillow and move to leave the clearing.

Wiggle your toes and fingers slightly. Flex your hands and arms. Feel yourself awakening.

Slowly open your eyes and let yourself adjust. You may stand up and stretch once you feel steady again.

Take what your guide told you and put it into practice. Show your love and appreciation for them.

Return to this meditation or ones similar to it frequently. Remember that time spent with your guide is time spent learning more about yourself.

CONCLUSION

The spiritual world is your oyster. You will reap what you sow. Respect and love is paid back in respect and love. As you grow, so shall your animal spirit guide. Someday you will look back and realize all the great things you have achieved together, because one day you decided to explore a part of your mind you had not looked at before. Once you put this book down, start on your journey. Whether this is your first foray or your 100th, go forth and explore your spirituality. You can grow and improve while bettering yourself and others in the process. You have so much potential ready to be harnessed. By following your heart and the wisdom of your guide, you can really start to make a change in the world.

CONCLUSION

We have gone over the history of animal spirit guides, learned about the people who believe in them, and how they have impacted our lives today. We have explored what an animal spirit guide is, the various types of guides we may encounter, and we have even elaborated on what some of the guides mean. We have discussed why we believe in animal spirit guides, how they can help us, and how we can include them in our lives. We have learned how to discover our guides and what they may mean for us as people. We have even learned how to meditate and talk with them. This was a journey for you, the reader, and for me, the writer. I have learned many things along the way in my research and I have been more than happy to share them all with you. Together we have grown, just as you and your guide shall grow in the future. Thank you for joining me in this adventure and good luck to you going forward.

REFERENCES

Ancient Celtic religion. (2020, April 26). https://en.wikipedia.org/wiki/Ancient_Celtic_religion

Ancient Egyptian religion. (2020, May 6). https://en.wikipedia.org/wiki/Ancient_Egyptian_religion#Animal_cults

Angel. (n.d.). *How to meditate properly to connect with your spirit guide.* The Guided Meditation Site. . https://www.the-guided-meditation-site.com/how-to-meditate-properly-to-connect-with-your-spirit-guide.html

Beauchesne, M. (2018, September 19). The Origination of the Spirit Animal. *Kheops International.* https://kheopsinternational.com/blog/origination-of-the-spirit-animal/

REFERENCES

Building Beautiful Souls. (n.d.). *Native American Zodiac*. https://www.buildingbeautifulsouls.com/zodiac-signs/native-american-zodiac-astrology/

Clarke, C. L. (n.d.). *How to Write a Guided Meditation Script*. The Guided Meditation Site. https://www.the-guided-meditation-site.com/write-a-guided-meditation.html

Dravidian folk religion. (2020, May 7). https://en.wikipedia.org/wiki/Dravidian_folk_religion

Dupre, B. (2018, April 5). *The Spiritual Importance of the Condor, Puma and Snake in Peruvian History*. Culture Trip. https://theculturetrip.com/south-america/peru/articles/the-spiritual-importance-of-the-condor-puma-and-snake-in-peruvian-history/

Fercility. (2020, March 31). *Chinese Zodiac*. China Highlights. https://www.chinahighlights.com/travelguide/chinese-zodiac/

Finnish paganism. (2020, April 25). https://en.wikipedia.org/wiki/Finnish_paganism

Hallett, K. (n.d.). *Why You Need to Find Your Spirit Animal*. Mind Body Network. https://mindbodynetwork.com/article/why-you-need-to-find-your-spirit-animal

Headspace. (n.d.) Meditation for beginners. https://www.headspace.com/meditation/meditation-for-beginners

Isakov, A. M. (n.d.). A Peruvian Shaman Shares 6 Spirit Animal Allies for Guidance, Healing and Wisdom. *The Shift Network.* https://blog.theshiftnetwork.com/blog/peruvian-shaman-shares-6-spirit-animal-allies-guidance-healing-wisdom

KaleidoSoul. (n.d.). *The Companions Suit- Your Animal Totems.* https://kaleidosoul.com/animal-totems.html

Katsanda, R. (2015, February 12). African Totems, Kinship and Conservation. *Wilderness Safaris.* https://wilderness-safaris.com/blog/posts/african-totems-kinship-and-conservation

Legends of America. (2020). *Native American Totem Animals & Their Meanings.* https://www.legendsofamerica.com/na-totems/

List of supernatural beings in Chinese folklore. (2020, March 22). https://en.wikipedia.org/wiki/List_of_supernatural_beings_in_Chinese_folklore

Lopez, D. (2019, June 7). *How to Find Your Animal*

REFERENCES

Spirit Guide. Exemplore. https://exemplore.com/spirit-animals/Finding-Your-Spirit-GuideAnimal-Totem

McCann, C. (n.d.). *A Guide to Spirit Animals.* Goop. https://goop.com/style/trends/guide-spirit-animals/

McCoy, D. (n.d.) *Totemism.* Norse Mythology for Smart People.

https://norse-mythology.org/concepts/totemism/

Mindworks Team. (n.d.). What is guided meditation? *Mindworks.* https://mindworks.org/blog/what-is-guided-meditation

Native Languages of the Americas. (n.d.) *Apache Legends and Myths.* http://www.native-languages.org/apache-legends.htm

Paulson, G. (n.d.). *Aboriginal spirituality.* Australians Together. https://australianstogether.org.au/discover/indigenous-culture/aboriginal-spirituality/

Psychic Library. (n.d.). *Animal Spirit Guides.* https://psychiclibrary.com/animal-spirit-guides/

Religion in Asia. (2020, May 3). https://en.wikipedia.org/wiki/Religion_in_Asia

Shaman Links. (n.d.). *Power Animals.* https://www.shamanlinks.net/shaman-info/the-spirit-world/power-animals/

Shirleytwofeathers. (n.d.). Celtic and Druid Spirit Animals. *The Powers That Be.* https://shirleytwofeathers.com/The_Blog/powers-that-be/celtic-and-druid-spirit-animals/

Sithole, J. (n.d.) *Zulu culture and cattle symbolism.* South Africa. https://www.southafrica.net/na/en/travel/article/zulu-culture-and-cattle-symbolism

The Editors of Encyclopaedia Britannica. (n.d.). *11 Egyptian Gods and Goddesses.* Encyclopaedia Britannica. https://www.britannica.com/list/11-egyptian-gods-and-goddesses

Traditional African religions. (2020, May 8). https://en.wikipedia.org/wiki/Traditional_African_religions

Ultimate Guide To Spirit Animals, Power Animals & Totems. (2019, October 28). https://www.spiritanimal.info/

REFERENCES

What is My Spirit Animal. (n.d.). *How to Find Your Spirit Animal - The Complete Guide.* https://whatismyspiritanimal.com/how-to-find-your-spirit-animal-complete-guide/#Meditation

www.ingramcontent.com/pod-product-compliance
Lightning Source LLC
Chambersburg PA
CBHW071911070526
44583CB00016B/1941